SALADS

SALADS

Over 60 satisfying salads for lunch and dinner

SUE QUINN
PHOTOGRAPHY BY VICTORIA WALL HARRIS

hardie grant books

CONTENTS

INTRODUCTION

Not only are salads good for your health, they can also be inventive and bold, and just as hearty as any cooked dish. They aren't difficult to make, but to be delicious they do need flavours to marry well. Use ingredients of the highest possible quality as in most cases you are going to eat them raw. So we recommend that you choose fruit and vegetables when they are at their best, which is when they are in season. Create harmony by combining different textures and flavours: a few soft dried fruits and crunchy seeds can make all the difference! And don't neglect your dressings. I have nothing against oil and vinegar, but why not try something a bit more original? A simple combination of diced vegetables can be transformed into an exceptional dish with the addition of a dressing with Asian flavours... You will find recipes for a variety of different salad dressings at the end of the book.

QUANTITIES

It can be difficult to gauge how much of each ingredient to use in a salad, so taste as you go along and adjust the quantities to your own liking. Add the dressing little by little and toss the salad with your fingertips; stop when the ingredients are lightly coated. If a handful of salad leaves or herbs does not seem enough, add more. These recipes are just guides. Some salads make better main dishes than others, but let your hunger be your guide as to how much to make.

SEASONAL INGREDIENTS

For most of the recipes, I recommend a season when the ingredients are at their best: when they have the most flavour and are easiest to get hold of.

STARCHY FOODS

DAIRY PRODUCTS, PROTEINS & FATS

FRUIT & VEGETABLES

THE ELEMENTS OF A SALAD

The salads in this book make complete, nutritionally balanced meals. They include the following ingredients.

STARCHY FOODS

These are an essential energy source. They contain nutrients such as fibre, calcium, iron and vitamin B. A salad should be made up of one third starchy foods such as pasta, noodles, bread, potatoes, couscous, quinoa, bulgur wheat, barley, rice, oats, rye, etc. Wherever possible use the wholegrain version.

FRUIT & VEGETABLES

A salad should consist of one third fruit and vegetables, canned, fresh, frozen or dried, to provide the necessary vitamins, minerals and fibre. Brightly coloured vegetables are important because they are rich in phytochemicals which help prevent cardiac diseases, cancers, cataracts and premature ageing. Green vegetables such as kale, Swiss chard, spinach, cabbage, watercress, romaine lettuce, broccoli and cauliflower are just as beneficial because they contain plenty of fibre and nutrients.

DAIRY PRODUCTS, PROTEINS & FATS

The final third of the salad should include at least one of each of the following ingredients, in moderate quantities:
• Cheese, yoghurt or dairy produce such as quark; excellent sources of protein and calcium.
• Meat, poultry, fish, eggs, tofu, beans or pulses; valuable sources of protein.
• Olive oil, avocado, nuts or seeds help lower cholesterol and are good sources of omega 3 essential fatty acids.

9

HOW TO CREATE A SALAD

Follow these steps to create a balanced salad.
To make a simpler salad, miss out step 9, or for a side dish, miss out step 3.
Don't forget, these are just guidelines!

1.

CHOOSE TOP-QUALITY VEGETABLES
Use lettuce or other leafy vegetables and/ or one or two key vegetables as a base.

2.

ADD STARCHY FOODS
Give this base body with the addition of starchy foods such as pasta, rice, bread, potatoes (skin on), couscous, quinoa, bulgur wheat, barley or rye.

3.

TO ENSURE A GOOD NUTRITIONAL BALANCE
Add a small amount of protein (meat, poultry, fish, eggs, tofu, pulses) and good-quality fats (olive oil, avocado, nuts and seeds). You can also sprinkle a little cheese onto your salad, but only after the dressing so that it doesn't disintegrate.

4.

ADD COLOUR
Add colourful fruit and vegetables such as diced red, yellow or green pepper, sweetcorn, tomatoes of various colours, grapes, pomegranate seeds or blueberries.

5.

ADD A FEW HIDDEN TREASURES
It's always nice to come across delicious surprises in a salad, so why not add some pieces of dried fruit or roasted hazelnuts?

10

6.

MAKE THE DRESSING

Fibre-rich vegetables such as kale need thicker dressings, while a light vinaigrette is more suitable for delicate salads. Liven up your vinaigrettes by adding herbs, chilli, capers, anchovies, olives, spices, crushed garlic or flavoured oils and vinegars.

7.

TOSS THE SALAD

Add the dressing, little by little, tossing it with the salad. Do this with your (clean) hands, it's the best way! Pour on enough dressing to coat the ingredients without drenching them.

8.

TEXTURE

The best salads have a bit of crunch, so add croutons, broken tortilla chips, crisps, savoury biscuits, or toasted cereals and nuts. Also try out our garnishes from the Dressings & Secret Toppings chapter, starting on p 151.

9.

A TOUCH OF GLAMOUR

Spruce up your salad with a few luxury ingredients for a glamorous touch. These pages are filled with suggestions to try, such as grated mullet roe, truffle or attractive young shoots and flowers.

11

PREPARING GRAINS & PULSES

GRAINS

QUINOA, SPELT, BARLEY, EINKORN,

WHEAT, ETC.

1. Rinse in plenty of cold water before cooking, then sauté in a little olive oil to bring out their flavour before putting on to boil.
2. Boil in salted water or stock, adding aromatic herbs such as bay leaves, onion and other herbs. Follow the instructions on the package for cooking times as these vary according to the grain.
3. Once cooked, rinse in cold water, drain and stir in a dash of olive oil to prevent the grains from sticking together. Spread them out on a large dish to cool and dry. You can also add the dressing when the grains are still warm and then let it all cool before adding crisp leaves, raw vegetables or cheese. Season generously as grains need to be well salted.

12

PULSES AND LENTILS

HARICOT BEANS, BLACK BEANS,

CHICKPEAS, GREEN AND BLACK PUY

LENTILS, ETC.

1. If you are using canned beans, rinse in plenty of cold water and drain well before adding a dressing or other ingredients.
2. If you are cooking them, rinse with plenty of cold water then leave to soak and/or cook according to the instructions on the package. Add salt once the beans or lentils are almost tender. Leave to simmer, then drain when cooked. To enhance their flavour, add the dressing while still warm, even if it is the day before. But allow to cool completely before adding ingredients such as crisp leaves, raw vegetables or cheese. Season generously as pulses and lentils need quite a lot of salt.

CUTTING THE VEGETABLES

USING A MANDOLINE

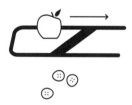

This is a very practical tool for cutting fruit, vegetables and hard cheeses into thin, regular slices. Many mandolines can be adjusted to produce different thicknesses of slice. Some even have interchangeable blades for cutting food into thin slices or julienne strips.

1. Place the mandoline on a flat work surface.
2. Make sure you hold it so that you are pushing the food away and not towards you or to the side.
3. Before you begin, round foods should be cut with a knife to create a flat surface to slice. For example, cut off the end of a courgette (zucchini).
4. Always use the 'pusher' to hold the food you are slicing because the blades of a mandoline are extremely sharp.
5. Apply regular pressure as you cut, holding the base of the mandoline in place with the other hand.

13

MAKING VEGETABLE STRIPS WITH A PEELER

1. Cut off the ends of the cucumber, carrot, courgette (zucchini) or other vegetable you want to cut into strips.
2. Place the vegetable on a flat work surface, parallel to you. Hold it firmly at one end and peel long ribbons by pressing firmly with the peeler from one end to the other.
3. If you are cutting a cucumber or courgette (zucchini), turn it over when you reach the seeds and peel the other side.

LEAVES, HERBS & FLOWERS

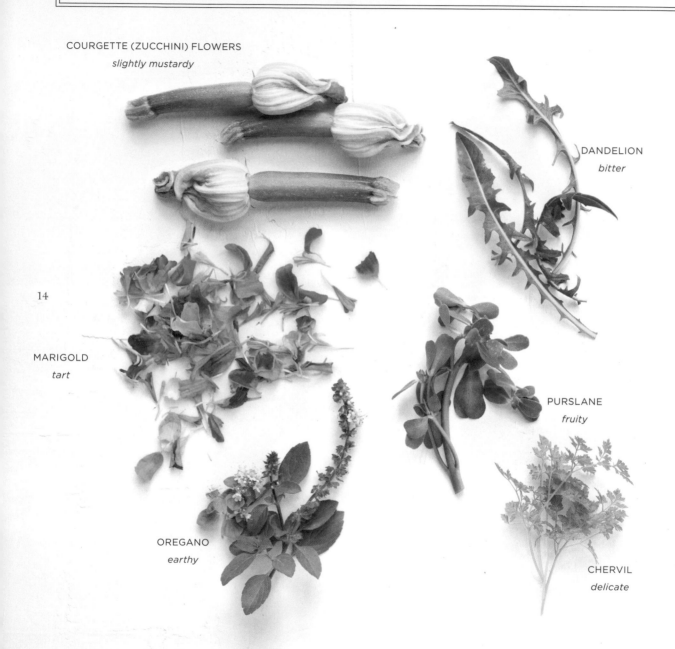

COURGETTE (ZUCCHINI) FLOWERS
slightly mustardy

DANDELION
bitter

14

MARIGOLD
tart

PURSLANE
fruity

OREGANO
earthy

CHERVIL
delicate

Transform a simple salad by adding these fabulous leaves, herbs and flowers. They're as pretty to look at as they are good for you.

CHARD
earthy

OAK LEAF LETTUCE
fresh

CAVOLO NERO
earthy

ROMAINE LETTUCE
sweet

SPINACH
earthy

KALE
earthy

BASIL
slightly peppery

LUXURY INGREDIENTS

GOAT'S CHEESE
slightly acid

FIGS
sweet

POMEGRANATE
fruity

16

PARMESAN
salty

NECTARINES
sweet

BURRATA
creamy

Garnish your most basic salad with a few glamorous ingredients which will give them flavour and an incomparable twist that will become your signature.

PUMPKIN SEEDS
buttery

GRATED MULLET ROE
iodised

PISTACHIOS
sweet

CHOPPED TRUFFLE
earthy

17

BARBERRIES
spicy

FLEUR DE SEL
mineral

SMOKED SALT
smoky

RED WALNUTS
salty

BLACK SALT
(KALA NAMAK)
pungent

GRAINS

& PULSES

Grains and pulses are excellent sources of protein that are
low in fat. They can make a light salad more substantial.
All our recipes use cooked dried grains and pulses, which you
need to prepare and allow to cool before making the salad.
Be generous with the seasoning and spices as grains and
pulses tend to absorb flavours.

GRAINS, BEETROOT & WALNUTS

serves 2–4

1 quantity of simple vinaigrette (p. 152)

1 teaspoon balsamic vinegar

2 teaspoons lemon zest, finely chopped

250 g (9 oz) cooked grain, such as spelt or pearl barley,
   drained and rinsed

1 small bunch of watercress (approximately 85 g/3 oz) with largest stalks removed

2 baby beetroots (approximately 200 g/7 oz) peeled and grated

salt and pepper

60 g (2½ oz) roasted walnuts, roughly chopped

method

Pour 2 tablespoons of vinaigrette into a salad bowl and mix with the balsamic vinegar
and lemon zest. Add the grains and watercress and toss to distribute the dressing.
Gently incorporate the beetroot then season with salt and
pepper to taste. Add more vinaigrette if necessary.
Sprinkle the walnuts on top and serve immediately.

SPICY QUINOA

serves 2–4

1 garlic clove, crushed

1 pinch chilli powder

1 medium red chilli, thinly sliced

1 quantity of simple vinaigrette (p. 152) replacing the vinegar
    with lemon juice

200g (7 oz) red quinoa, cooked and rinsed

250 g (9 oz) cooked or canned haricot (navy) beans, drained and rinsed

1 handful of coriander (cilantro), chopped

1 handful of flat-leaf parsley, chopped

3 tablespoons pumpkin seeds

1 avocado

lime juice, as desired

method

Add the garlic, chilli powder and sliced chilli to the vinaigrette.
Put the quinoa, haricot beans, herbs and pumpkin seeds into a salad
bowl. Pour over enough dressing to coat the ingredients.
Peel and de-stone the avocado, cut it into chunks, and incorporate it into the salad.
Add lime juice to taste, and more dressing if necessary. Serve immediately.

GREEN TABBOULEH

serves 2–4

80 g (3 oz) cooked grain, such as barley, spelt,
  or einkorn wheat

200 g (7 oz) nicely ripe assorted tomatoes, quartered

100 g (3½ oz) cucumber in fine rounds

½ red onion, finely chopped

45 ml (2 fl oz) lemon juice, or more as desired

2 teaspoons Ras el Hanout spice mix or ground coriander

50 g (2 oz) flat-leaf parsley, finely chopped

1 handful of purslane, chopped

25 g (1 oz) mint leaves, finely snipped

45 ml (2 fl oz) extra-virgin olive oil, or more as desired

salt and pepper

method

Put the grain, tomatoes, cucumber and onion into a salad bowl.
Add the lemon juice, Ras el Hanout, herbs, olive oil and season with salt and pepper.
Toss gently and add extra lemon juice, olive oil, salt and pepper, as desired.
Set aside for 20 minutes to allow the flavours to mingle before serving.

BORLOTTI BEANS WITH GREEN VEGETABLES

26

serves 2–4

240 g (9 oz) cooked or canned borlotti beans, drained and rinsed

80 g (3 oz) French beans, stalks removed, finely chopped

100 g (3½ oz) cucumber, thinly sliced

a handful of rocket leaves

½ a large red onion, finely chopped

1 blood orange, peeled and membrane removed, cut into slices

50 g (2 oz) green olives, pitted and chopped

2 quantities of simple vinaigrette (p. 152) replacing the vinegar with orange juice
    and replacing the vegetable oil with olive oil

method

Put all the ingredients, except the dressing, into a large salad bowl. Pour half the
dressing on top and toss gently. Add more dressing to taste. Serve immediately.

QUEEN OF SHEBA

serves 2–4

1 quantity of Middle Eastern dressing (p. 158)

300 g (11 oz) cooked grains, for example bulgur wheat,
    pearl barley, spelt or a mixture, rinsed and drained

1 handful of dried cherries or barberries

4 tablespoons toasted flaked almonds

1 generous handful of flat-leaf parsley, coarsely chopped

1 generous handful of mint leaves, coarsely snipped

2 teaspoons grated lemon zest

salt and pepper

the seeds of ½ a pomegranate

method

Warm the dressing in a small saucepan over a low heat.
Add 3 tablespoons of dressing to the grain. Allow to cool.
Add the other ingredients to the grain, except for the pomegranate seeds.
Toss, then add some dressing or salt and pepper to taste.
Sprinkle with pomegranate seeds just before serving.

LENTILS, CHERRIES & ROCKET

30

serves 2–4

2 quantities of simple vinaigrette (p. 152) made with balsamic vinegar

1 garlic clove, peeled and crushed

2 teaspoons honey

500 g (1 lb 2 oz) Puy lentils, cooked, rinsed and drained

350 g (12 oz) cherries, pitted and quartered

1 generous handful of salad leaves, such as rocket,
    mizuna or dandelion

salt and pepper

method

Mix the vinaigrette, garlic and honey.
In a shallow dish, stir together the lentils, cherries, salad leaves
and enough dressing to coat the ingredients.
Season generously with salt and pepper and serve immediately.

TOMATOES & CREAMY LENTILS

serves 2–4

2 quantities of yoghurt dressing (p. 154)

4 tablespoons flat-leaf parsley or coriander (cilantro), snipped

salt and pepper

450 g (1 lb) lentils, cooked, rinsed and drained

300 g (11 oz) nicely ripe tomatoes, diced

2 handfuls of baby spinach leaves, chopped

1 generous dash of lemon juice, or more as desired

method

Mix together the dressing, herbs, and season with salt and pepper. Put the lentils into
a salad bowl and pour over enough dressing to coat them generously. Incorporate the
tomatoes and spinach leaves. Add lemon juice, and extra salt and pepper to taste. If you
have time, set aside for 30 minutes before serving to allow the flavours to mingle.

MEDITERRANEAN TABBOULEH

serves 2–4

½ garlic clove, crushed

2 quantities of simple vinaigrette (p. 152) made with balsamic vinegar

350 g (12 oz) Israeli couscous, cooked

80 g (3 oz) red (bell) peppers marinated in oil, drained and diced

80 g (3 oz) artichoke hearts marinated in oil, drained and diced

80 g (3 oz) aubergines (eggplant) marinated in oil, drained and diced

60 g (2½ oz) red tomatoes marinated in oil, drained and halved

45 g (1½ oz) capers, coarsely chopped

40 g (1½ oz) black olives, pitted

1 handful of basil leaves, torn

salt and pepper

1 dash of lemon juice

method

Add the garlic to the vinaigrette. Arrange all the other ingredients in
a salad bowl and coat them generously with dressing.
Season with salt, pepper and lemon juice to taste. Set aside for
20 minutes before serving to allow the flavours to mingle.

TUNA & HARICOT BEANS

36

serves 2–4

500 g (1 lb 2 oz) cooked or
    canned haricot (navy) beans,
    rinsed and drained
300 g (11 oz) albacore tuna
    in oil (drained weight)
1 red onion, finely chopped
3 anchovy fillets in oil, drained
15 g flat-leaf parsley
10 g (⅓ oz) basil leaves
5 sage leaves
1 tablespoon capers
1 garlic clove
135 ml (4½ fl oz) extra-virgin olive oil
½ teaspoon Dijon mustard
salt and pepper
1 tablespoon lemon juice, or more as desired

method

Place the haricot beans, tuna and onion in a large dish. Put the other ingredients into
the bowl of a food processor and blend until you have a fairly thick dressing.
Incorporate the dressing into the bean mixture then season with salt and pepper and lemon
juice to taste. Set aside for 30 minutes before serving to allow the flavours to mingle.

QUINOA WITH PESTO & FETA

38

serves 2–4

3 quantities of simple vinaigrette (p. 152)

3 tablespoons pesto, or more as desired

450 g (1 lb) red or white quinoa, cooked, rinsed and drained

3 spring onions (scallions), finely chopped

15 g (½ oz) coriander (cilantro), snipped

15 g (½ oz) dill, chopped

15 g (½ oz) mint leaves, snipped

4 tablespoons pine kernels, toasted

75 g (3 oz) feta

salt and pepper

method

Mix the vinaigrette and pesto. Gently mix the quinoa, spring onions,
herbs, and half the feta together in a salad bowl.
Pour over enough of the dressing to coat the ingredients, season with salt and pepper. Sprinkle
the remaining feta and the pine kernels on top. Add more salt and pepper or dressing to taste.

SOBA NOODLES WITH MISO DRESSING

serves 2-4

200 g (7 oz) cooked
  soba noodles (cold)

1 dash of toasted sesame oil

2 generous handfuls of assorted baby salad leaves

100 g (3½ oz) carrots, grated

90 g (3 oz) raw sweetcorn

1 avocado, peeled and cut into chunks

2 spring onions (scallions)

2 handfuls of coriander (cilantro), snipped

30 g (1 oz) sunflower seeds

½ tablespoon black sesame seeds

1 quantity of miso and ginger dressing (p. 164)

1 dash of lemon juice

salt and pepper

method

Mix the noodles with the sesame oil to prevent them from sticking. Place them in a
large salad bowl with the baby salad leaves, vegetables, coriander and seeds.
Pour over enough dressing to coat the ingredients generously. Add a dash
of lemon juice, salt and pepper to taste. Serve immediately.

FALAFELS WITH SALAD

serves 2–4

3 tablespoons tahini

2 tablespoons lemon juice, or more as desired

½ garlic clove, crushed

salt and pepper

150 g (5 oz) cherry tomatoes, halved

100 g (3½ oz) cooked or canned chickpeas, rinsed and drained

150 g (5 oz) cucumbers, halved and thinly sliced

2 generous handfuls of assorted salad leaves

2 small handfuls of flat-leaf parsley

1 or 2 pitta breads, toasted and cut into large pieces

6 falafels, halved

method

Mix the tahini, lemon juice, garlic and season with salt and pepper. Add 50–100 ml
(2–4 fl oz) cold water to make a dressing that is still quite thick. Arrange all the other
ingredients, except for the pitta bread and falafels, in a large salad bowl.
Pour over enough dressing to coat the ingredients, then add salt, pepper
and lemon juice to taste. Top with the pitta bread and falafels just
before serving, and serve the remaining dressing separately.

BEANS & PEPPERS WITH CHILLI

44

serves 2–4

½ teaspoon chilli powder

2 quantities of Middle Eastern dressing (p. 158)
    replacing the lemon juice with lime juice

450 g (1 lb) cooked or canned beans, such as black beans,
    kidney beans or haricot (navy) beans, drained and rinsed

1 red (bell) pepper, diced

1 green (bell) pepper, diced

1 red onion, finely chopped

30 g (1 oz) coriander (cilantro), snipped

lime juice, as desired

salt and pepper

method

Mix the chilli powder into the dressing.
Put all the other ingredients, except for the lime juice, salt and pepper, into a salad bowl.
Pour over enough of the dressing to coat the ingredients well. Add lime juice,
salt and pepper to taste. Set aside for 30 minutes before serving.

PROTEIN

These energy-packed salads can make excellent main dishes or delicious starters. Some are so special they would not be out of place at a festive occasion. They all contain ingredients that are delightful to eat as well as being satisfying and healthy.

SUPER ENERGY

48

serves 2–4

350 g (12 oz) mixed quinoa, cooked

120 g (4 oz) broccoli in small florets

80 g (3 oz) different-coloured carrots, grated or in julienne strips

2 handfuls of baby spinach leaves

2 handfuls of baby kale leaves

2 quantities of yuzu dressing (p. 162)

chilli powder, as desired

salt and pepper

180 g (6 oz) tofu, baked in the oven or fried, cut into dice
   (hot or at room temperature)

method

Arrange the quinoa and all the vegetables in a large salad bowl. Pour over enough
dressing to coat the ingredients well. Add chilli powder, salt and pepper to taste.
Set aside for 20 minutes to allow the flavours to mingle.
Sprinkle the tofu on top and serve immediately. Serve the remaining dressing separately.

MACKEREL & SAMPHIRE

50

serves 2–4

150 g (5 oz) samphire, cut unto sections

200 g (7 oz) cucumber

1 generous handful of assorted baby salad leaves

40 g (1½ oz) gherkins (dill pickles), halved

20 g (¾ oz) capers

1 preserved lemon, pulp removed, skin finely sliced

3 tablespoons extra-virgin olive oil

black pepper

2 fillets of smoked mackerel, weighing approximately 70 g (2¼ oz) each,
    skin removed, flesh flaked

2 tablespoons lemon juice, or more as desired

method

Put the samphire, cucumber, salad leaves, gherkins, capers and preserved lemon
in a salad bowl. Pour the olive oil and lemon juice on top. Add pepper.
Gently incorporate the mackerel into the salad and add lemon juice to taste.
Arrange the salad on individual plates and serve immediately.

PRAWN & GRAPE

serves 2–4

1 quantity of yoghurt dressing
  (p. 154) without cumin
80 g (3 oz) cucumber, grated
20 small or 10 large basil leaves, finely chopped
2 tablespoons lemon juice, or more as desired
160 g (5½ oz) cooked prawns (shrimp), weight with heads and shells removed
100 g (3½ oz) black seedless grapes
100 g (3½ oz) canned or cooked chickpeas, rinsed and drained
100 g (3½ oz) yellow (bell) pepper, diced
10 romaine lettuce leaves, finely sliced
salt and pepper

best in autumn

53

method

Mix the dressing, cucumber, basil and half the lemon juice.
Place all the other ingredients in a salad bowl.
Pour over enough dressing to coat the ingredients and toss gently.
Add lemon juice, salt and pepper to taste. Serve immediately.

CALIFORNIA SALAD

serves 2–4

4 large or 8 small romaine lettuce leaves, finely sliced

4 cavolo nero leaves, central rib removed, finely sliced

150 g (5 oz) cooked chicken, thinly sliced

8 assorted cherry tomatoes, halved

80 g (3 oz) raw sweetcorn kernels

1 slice of streaky bacon, diced and grilled

2 hardboiled eggs, halved

1 avocado

60 g (2½ oz) goat's cheese, crumbled

2 quantities of simple vinaigrette (p. 152) made with red wine vinegar

½ tablespoon honey or agave syrup

method

Lay the lettuce and cavolo nero on a serving dish or on separate plates, then
arrange the chicken, tomatoes, sweetcorn, bacon and eggs on top.
Dice the avocado and add it to the salad. Finish by sprinkling the goat's cheese on top.
Mix the vinaigrette and honey (or agave syrup), and pour on top, to taste. Serve immediately.

KALE CAESAR SALAD

serves 2–4

400 g (14 oz) assorted kale leaves, central rib removed,
   finely chopped
4 tablespoons olive oil
1 garlic clove
3 quantities of anchovy dressing (p. 166)
120 g (4 oz) herby croutons (p. 174)
40 g (1½ oz) grated Parmesan

*best in
autumn and
winter*

method

Place the kale leaves in a small salad bowl, add the olive oil and let
it seep in to soften the kale. Set aside for 10 minutes.
Rub the sides of a salad bowl with a clove of garlic then pour in three-quarters
of the dressing. Add the kale and the croutons and toss to coat them. Add more
dressing if necessary. Sprinkle with Parmesan and serve immediately.

BROAD BEANS, RICOTTA & PEACHES

serves 2–4

300 g (11 oz) ricotta
½ teaspoon smoked salt, or more as desired
3 tablespoons extra-virgin olive oil
2 generous handfuls of assorted baby salad leaves
4 large or 6 small peaches cut into thin wedges
250 g (9 oz) fresh or frozen broad (fava) beans, blanched, skins removed
the juice of one lime, or more as desired
salt and pepper

method

Whisk the ricotta with the smoked salt and 1 tablespoon of olive oil.
Arrange the salad leaves, peaches and broad beans
in a dish. Add the remaining olive oil and the lime juice.
Sprinkle the whisked ricotta or add it in balls. Add salt, pepper
and lime juice to taste. Serve immediately.

FRISÉE, POACHED EGG & DUKKAH

serves 2–4

4 generous handfuls of frisée lettuce

4 quantities of simple vinaigrette (p. 152) made with sherry vinegar

salt and pepper

4 poached eggs

200 g (7 oz) cooked diced bacon

4 tablespoons dukkah (p. 178)

method

Toss the frisée lettuce with half of the vinaigrette, then season with salt and pepper.
Share out into separate shallow bowls. Top the salad with one
or two poached eggs and a few cubes of bacon.
Pour the remaining dressing on top and sprinkle with dukkah. Serve immediately.

SWEETCORN & RADICCHIO

62

serves 2–4

1 quantity of simple vinaigrette (p. 152) made with lemon juice

1 heaped tablespoon grated Parmesan

1 teaspoon honey

1 radicchio halved, scooped out and sliced

the uncooked kernels of two corns on the cob

100 g (3½ oz) smoked ham, diced

3 tablespoons herbs, such as flat-leaf parsley,
    dill, basil, chives, or a mixture, snipped

method

Mix the vinaigrette, Parmesan and honey. Arrange the
radicchio, sweetcorn and ham in a salad bowl.
Pour over enough dressing to coat the ingredients.
Gently incorporate the herbs and serve immediately.

CRAB, RADISH & FENNEL

64

serves 2

120 ml (4 fl oz) white wine vinegar

2 teaspoons caster (superfine) sugar

salt

60 g (2 oz) fennel bulbs, finely sliced

60 ml (2 fl oz) chilli oil

2 tablespoons lemon juice

pepper

250 g (9 oz) cooked or canned crab meat, crumbled

1 bunch of watercress (approximately 30 g/1 oz), sliced,
    large stalks removed

2 small radishes or 1 large radish cut into thin rounds

edible marigold petals, for decoration (optional)

method

Mix the vinegar, sugar and a pinch of salt in a bowl, then add the fennel and leave to marinate for
30 minutes. Drain and remove the excess liquid. Mix the chilli
oil, lemon juice and season with salt and pepper.
Share out the crab meat onto separate plates and add a dash of chilli dressing
on top. Add the watercress, radish and fennel, then toss. Pour the remaining
dressing over and sprinkle a few flowers, if using, on top before serving.

PEAS, HAM & PECORINO

66

serves 2–4

4 tablespoons lemon juice

120 ml (4 fl oz) extra-virgin olive oil

160 g (5½ oz) pea shoots

160 g (5½ oz) fresh peas, uncooked

200 g (7 oz) cooked smoked ham, diced

pepper

100 g (3½ oz) pecorino cheese in thin flakes

method

Combine the lemon juice and olive oil. Arrange the pea shoots, peas and ham in a dish.
Pour over enough dressing to coat them, season with pepper and sprinkle with pecorino.
Serve immediately.

WALDORF SALAD WITH CHICKEN

68

serves 2–4

100 g (3½ oz) Greek-style yoghurt

1 tablespoon tarragon, chopped

1 tablespoon lemon juice

salt and pepper

3 medium chicken breasts, cooked and thinly sliced

2 sticks of celery, thinly sliced

1 red apple, cut into matchsticks

150 g (5 oz) black seedless grapes, halved

50 g (2 oz) toasted walnut kernels, halved

2 handfuls of crisp salad leaves, torn if large

method

Whisk together the yoghurt, tarragon and lemon juice. Season with salt and pepper.
Place all the other ingredients, except the salad leaves, in a bowl.
Pour enough of the yoghurt dressing over the chicken mixture to generously coat the ingredients.
Put the salad leaves into a salad bowl and top with the chicken mixture. Serve immediately.

FIGS, COPPA HAM & BURRATA

70

serves 2

90 ml (3 fl oz) extra-virgin olive oil

45 ml (1½ fl oz) balsamic vinegar

salt and pepper

4 handfuls of salad leaves, such as rocket (arugula),
   mizuna or young shoots

6 figs, halved

8 slices coppa ham

1 large ball or 2 small balls of burrata

3 tablespoons pistachios, crushed

method

Combine the oil, vinegar and season with salt and pepper. Place the salad
leaves in a dish and arrange the figs and coppa ham on top.
Add the burrata to the dish, either as a ball, or halved.
Add dressing to taste and sprinkle with pistachios. Serve immediately.

AUBERGINE, LABNEH & POMEGRANATE

72

serves 2–4

2 quantities of simple vinaigrette (p. 152)

2 tablespoons pomegranate molasses

2 teaspoons za'atar

400 g (14 oz) grilled aubergines (eggplant) in oil, drained and diced

1 generous handful of mint leaves, coarsely chopped

1 generous handful of flat-leaf parsley, coarsely chopped

160 g (5½ oz) labneh or goat's curd cheese, or more as desired

the seeds of ½ a pomegranate

method

Mix the vinaigrette with the pomegranate molasses and za'atar.
Place the aubergines and herbs in a dish then pour over enough dressing to coat them.
Add the labneh and sprinkle with pomegranate seeds. Serve immediately.

TROPICAL PRAWNS

74

serves 2-4

300 g (11 oz) prawns (shrimp), cooked and shelled

150 g (5 oz) cucumber, deseeded and diced

1 mango, flesh scooped out and cut into matchsticks

8 to 12 crisp salad leaves, such as romaine

1 handful of mint leaves, snipped

1 handful of coriander (cilantro), chopped

1 medium red chilli, thinly sliced

1 quantity of Thai vinaigrette (p. 156)

method

Gently mix all the ingredients, except for the dressing, in a shallow dish.
Pour over enough dressing to coat the ingredients. Serve immediately.

MULLET ROE, CELERY & EGGS

76

serves 2–4

6 celery sticks, cut diagonally

4 handfuls of flat-leaf parsley leaves

2 handfuls of salad leaves

2 quantities of simple vinaigrette (p. 152)

4 soft-boiled eggs

4 tablespoons toasted hazelnuts, crushed

4 tablespoons dried breadcrumbs

4 tablespoons pressed mullet roe, grated, or more as desired

method

Divide the celery, parsley and salad leaves between shallow
dishes and add enough dressing to coat them.
Arrange the eggs on top and sprinkle with hazelnuts, breadcrumbs and fish roe.
Serve immediately.

SMOKED SALMON & SPELT

serves 2–4

240 ml (8 fl oz) cider vinegar

2 tablespoons caster (superfine) sugar

160 g (5½ oz) cucumber, halved then finely sliced

1 small red onion, halved then finely chopped

320 g (11 oz) spelt or pearl barley, cooked and rinsed

12 cherry tomatoes, halved

4 tablespoons extra-virgin olive oil

2 tablespoons lemon juice, or more as desired

160 g (5½ oz) slices of smoked salmon, cut into thin strips

2 tablespoons chopped dill, plus a few sprigs to garnish

salt and pepper

method

In a salad bowl, mix the vinegar with the sugar, then add
the cucumber and onion. Set aside for 30 minutes then drain.
Put the spelt or barley and the tomatoes in a shallow dish.
Add the olive oil and lemon juice, followed by the smoked salmon, the drained cucumber
and onion, and finally the dill. Add extra lemon juice and salt and pepper to taste.
Sprinkle a few sprigs of dill on top and serve immediately.

SALADE NIÇOISE

80

serves 2–4

2 quantities of simple vinaigrette (p. 152)
    made with red wine vinegar

1 garlic clove, peeled and crushed

leaves of 2 little gem lettuces

4 nicely ripe plum tomatoes, plunged into hot water
    to remove the skins, and quartered

2 hard-boiled eggs, halved

½ cucumber, halved and then sliced into strips

4 artichoke hearts in oil, drained

10 black olives

8 anchovy fillets in oil, drained

1 small handful of basil leaves, torn

method

Mix the vinaigrette and garlic. Place the lettuce leaves, tomatoes,
eggs, cucumber, artichokes, olives and anchovies in a dish.
Pour the dressing on top and sprinkle with basil leaves. Serve immediately.

NECTARINE & LARDO DI COLONNATA

82

serves 2–4

3 ripe nectarines, cut into narrow segments
2 generous handfuls of rocket (arugula)
60 g (2 oz) yellow French beans, destalked
   and cut into thin diagonal strips
2 quantities of simple vinaigrette (p. 152)
4 to 6 slices of white lardo di colonnata
   (cured pork fat) cut into large pieces

method

Arrange the nectarines, rocket and beans in a dish and pour
over enough vinaigrette to coat the ingredients.
Place the lardo di colonnata on top. Serve immediately.

ROQUEFORT, PEAR, CELERY & WALNUTS

84

serves 2–4

2 tablespoons lemon juice

60 ml (2 fl oz) hazelnut oil

½ teaspoon salt, plus extra to season

2 fresh pears

3 sticks of celery, thinly sliced

120 g (4 oz) walnut kernels

180 g (6 oz) Roquefort, crumbled

pepper

method

Whisk the lemon juice, hazelnut oil and salt together in a large salad bowl.
Core the pears and cut into thin strips. Add them to the salad
bowl, along with the celery and walnuts. Toss gently.
Incorporate the cheese, season with pepper, then add salt if necessary.
Share out onto separate plates and serve immediately.

CHORIZO, PEPPER & CHICKPEAS

serves 2–4

½ teaspoon smoked paprika

1 garlic clove, peeled and crushed

2 quantities of simple vinaigrette (p. 152) made with sherry vinegar
    and olive oil instead of the vegetable oil/olive oil mixture

300 g (11 oz) cooked or canned chickpeas, rinsed and drained

200 g (7 oz) chorizo, skin removed, halved lengthwise,
    then finely sliced

120 g (4 oz) red peppers marinated in oil, drained and diced

20 g (¾ oz) flat-leaf parsley, snipped

salt and pepper

method

Add the paprika and garlic to the vinaigrette. Place all the other ingredients in a
salad bowl. Pour over enough of the dressing to coat the ingredients well.
Set aside for 20 minutes before serving.

COURGETTE & GOAT'S CHEESE

88

serves 2–4

500 g (1 lb 2 oz) assorted courgettes
   (zucchini), thinly sliced
2 tablespoons yuzu or lemon juice
90 ml (3 fl oz) extra-virgin olive oil
1 garlic clove, crushed
the leaves of 3 sprigs of thyme, chopped
salt and pepper
80 g (3 oz) goat's cheese or curd
2 tablespoons toasted pine kernels
1 small handful of basil leaves, torn
the grated zest of ½ a lemon, finely chopped

method

Mix the courgettes, yuzu or lemon juice, olive oil, garlic and thyme,
then season with salt and pepper. Set aside for 30 minutes.
Drain, set aside the dressing and arrange the courgettes in a dish.
Sprinkle with goat's cheese, pine kernels, basil and lemon zest. Add
a dash of the reserved dressing to taste. Serve cool.

BEETROOT & GOAT'S CHEESE

serves 2–4

1 red onion, halved and sliced thinly

1 tablespoon chopped tarragon, plus a few leaves for garnish

1 quantity of simple vinaigrette (p. 152)

250 g (9 oz) cooked beetroots, in fine strips

250 g (9 oz) fresh soft goat's cheese or crumbled goat's cheese

pepper

method

Steep the onion in water for 10 minutes, then drain and dab off any
excess liquid. Add the chopped tarragon to the vinaigrette.
Arrange the beetroot, onion and cheese in a dish.
Pour the dressing on top, then sprinkle with tarragon leaves
and season with pepper. Serve immediately.

DUCK, ORANGE & WALNUTS

serves 2

3 tablespoons walnut oil

2 tablespoons sherry vinegar

1 dash of orange blossom water

the zest and juice of ½ an orange

100 g (3½ oz) duck confit, shredded

20 g (¾ oz) walnuts, toasted and crushed

1 orange, peeled and membrane removed, cut into rounds

10 small leaves of red endive

1 handful of sorrel

salt and pepper

method

Combine the oil, vinegar, orange blossom water, orange zest
and juice. Arrange the other ingredients in a dish.
Pour over enough dressing to coat the ingredients. Season with
salt and pepper to taste. Serve immediately.

RADISH, PEAS & RICOTTA

94

serves 2–4

1 quantity of simple vinaigrette (p. 152)

1 tablespoon hazelnut oil

250 g (9 oz) radishes, cut into fine strips, ideally with a mandoline

60 g (2 oz) pea shoots

1 handful of raw peas

lemon juice to taste

salt and pepper

200 g (7 oz) ricotta, thinly sliced or crumbled

method

Combine the vinaigrette and hazelnut oil. Arrange the radishes,
pea shoots and peas in a dish. Add the vinaigrette.
Season with salt and pepper, and add lemon juice to taste.
Sprinkle with ricotta and serve immediately.

CAPRESE SALAD

serves 2–4

800 g (1 lb 10 oz) tomatoes of varying ripeness
salt
2 large balls of buffalo mozzarella or burrata
1 handful of assorted basil
pepper
a dash of olive oil

97

method

Cut the tomatoes into thin crosswise slices. Sprinkle with salt and arrange on a dish.
Tear the mozzarella or burrata into pieces and add to the tomatoes. Arrange
the basil leaves on top, add salt if necessary, and season with pepper.
Pour a dash of oil on top and serve immediately.

GREEK SALAD

serves 2–4

½ red onion, thinly sliced

2 quantities of simple vinaigrette (p. 152) made with red wine vinegar
     and olive oil instead of the vegetable/olive oil mixture

250 g (9 oz) ripe tomatoes, diced

salt

1 medium cucumber, diced

20 black olives, pitted

2 heaped tablespoons chopped oregano

150 g (5 oz) feta

1 preserved lemon, pulp removed, skin thinly sliced (optional)

pepper

method

Allow the onion to steep in the vinaigrette for 20 minutes, then drain, keeping the dressing.
Arrange the tomatoes in a dish and sprinkle with salt. Add the cucumber, olives,
oregano and onion. Pour over enough vinaigrette to coat the ingredients.
Crumble the feta on top and sprinkle with preserved lemon, if
using, and season with pepper. Serve immediately.

LOBSTER, TRUFFLE & ASPARAGUS

100

serves 2–4

100 ml (3 fl oz) mayonnaise (p. 160)

a few drops of truffle oil, or as desired

2 lobster tails, steamed, shelled
   and cut into medallions

2 tablespoons olive oil

80 g (3 oz) asparagus tips, thinly cut lengthwise

4 small handfuls of baby salad leaves or shoots

salt and pepper

200 g (7 oz) new potatoes, steamed
   and cut into rounds

a generous dash of lemon juice

black truffle, grated

method

Combine the mayonnaise with the truffle oil and a splash of water.
Coat the lobster tails with 2 tablespoons of mayonnaise and share them out onto separate plates.
Pour a dash of olive oil over the asparagus and salad leaves, then season
with salt and pepper. Arrange them on the lobster tails.
Coat the potatoes with 2 tablespoons of mayonnaise and arrange them around
the lobster. Pour on the remaining mayonnaise and some lemon juice.
Sprinkle with grated truffle before serving.

VEGETABLES

These recipes show that a salad consisting solely of vegetables can be absolutely delicious. Use the finest ingredients you can get hold of and, for best results, add the dressing just before serving (unless indicated otherwise).

ALL GREEN SALAD

104

serves 2–4

2 quantities of simple vinaigrette (p. 152)

1 handful of assorted baby salad leaves, such as rocket (arugula), mizuna, dandelion,
    sorrel, watercress, or young shoots, mixed with a few herbs

4 handfuls of lettuce leaves

salt and pepper

enjoy all year round!

method

Pour half the vinaigrette into a big salad bowl, then add the salad
leaves and herbs. Toss gently to coat with dressing.
Add salt, pepper and more dressing to taste. Serve immediately.

SPICY AVOCADO & BUTTERNUT SQUASH

106

serves 2–4

400 g (14 oz) butternut squash, peeled, deseeded and grated

25 g (1 oz) pumpkin seeds

2 quantities of lime and chilli dressing (p. 168)

2 avocados

salt and pepper

method

Place the squash and pumpkin seeds in a salad bowl, then pour over enough dressing
to coat them generously. Season with salt and pepper and set aside for 10 minutes.
Peel the avocados, remove the stones and cut the flesh into small chunks.
Add the avocado to the squash and add more dressing. Toss gently.
Season with salt and pepper to taste. Serve immediately.

TOMATO, SPINACH & RASPBERRY

serves 2–4

1 tablespoon raspberry vinegar

1½ tablespoons hazelnut oil

1½ tablespoons olive oil

salt and pepper

300 g (11 oz) assorted tomatoes, diced

60 g (2 oz) baby spinach leaves

thyme muesli (p. 182)

method

Combine the vinegar, oils and season with salt and pepper.
Arrange the tomatoes and spinach in a dish.
Pour over enough dressing to coat the ingredients.
Sprinkle with thyme muesli and serve immediately.

CUCUMBER & CASHEW NUTS

serves 2–4

3 assorted small cucumbers, cut into thin rounds,
  ideally using a mandoline

1 large pinch of salt

50 g (2 oz) toasted cashew nuts, roughly chopped

1 tablespoon vegetable oil

2 tablespoons lime juice

½ tablespoon caster (superfine) sugar

2 teaspoons nuoc mâm fish sauce

1 red chilli, finely chopped

½ garlic clove, crushed

best in summer

method

Arrange the cucumber rounds in a colander and sprinkle with salt. Leave for 30 minutes to draw out the water. Dab off any excess liquid and put the rounds into a dish with half the cashew nuts. Mix all the other ingredients, except for the remaining cashew nuts, to make a dressing and pour enough of this over the cucumber to coat it. Sprinkle the remaining cashew nuts on top and serve immediately.

FENNEL & GRAPEFRUIT

serves 2–4

1 quantity of simple vinaigrette (p. 152)

2 teaspoons honey

2 pink grapefruits, peeled and membrane removed, cut into rounds

2 medium fennel bulbs, hard part removed, halved
    then finely sliced, keeping the leaves

20 g (¾ oz) toasted almonds, roughly chopped

salt and pepper

fennel flowers (optional)

method

Mix the vinaigrette and the honey. Arrange the grapefruit, fennel bulbs and most
of the almonds in a shallow bowl. Pour over enough dressing to coat them.
Season with salt and pepper to taste. Sprinkle with the remaining
almonds, fennel leaves and flowers, if using. Serve immediately.

TOMATO, ONION & PEPPER

114

serves 2

325 g (11 oz) cherry tomatoes, halved

½ cucumber, deseeded and finely sliced

1 green (bell) pepper, finely chopped

1 red onion, finely chopped

2 tablespoons coriander (cilantro), finely snipped

2 tablespoons mint, finely snipped

1 red chilli, finely sliced

salt and pepper

1 quantity of Middle-Eastern dressing (p. 158)

lemon juice, to taste

method

Place all the ingredients, except for the dressing, lemon juice and seasoning
in a large salad bowl. Pour over enough dressing to coat them.
Taste and season with salt and pepper or lemon juice, as desired. Serve immediately.

MARINATED KALE

serves 2–4

4 quantities of simple vinaigrette (p. 152)

1½ tablespoons honey

1 teaspoon chilli powder, or as desired

the zest of an orange, finely chopped

200 g (7 oz) assorted kale, central rib removed, finely chopped

60 g (2 oz) hulled hazelnuts, toasted and roughly chopped

116

method

Mix the vinaigrette with the honey, chilli powder and orange zest.
Pour into a salad bowl. Add the kale and toss to coat.
Leave to marinate for at least 1 hour. Sprinkle with hazelnuts before serving.

RAW CABBAGE WITH CUMIN

118

serves 2–4

2 quantities of simple vinaigrette (p. 152)
    made with red wine vinegar

2 tablespoons cumin seeds, lightly crushed

200 g (7 oz) red cabbage, finely sliced

2 carrots (approximately 120 g/4 oz),
    sliced into julienne strips

1 crunchy red apple

salt and pepper

method

Mix the vinaigrette with the cumin seeds. Place the cabbage and carrots in a large salad bowl.
Core the apple then cut it into julienne strips, leaving the skin on, and add to the salad bowl.
Pour over enough dressing to coat the ingredients, then season with salt and pepper to taste.
Set aside for 20 minutes before serving to allow the flavours to mingle.

CAULIFLOWER TABBOULEH

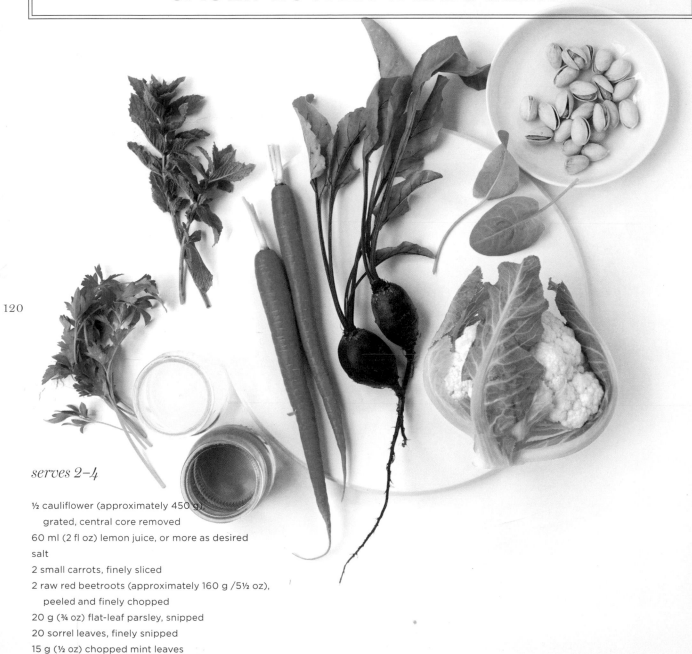

serves 2–4

½ cauliflower (approximately 450 g),
    grated, central core removed
60 ml (2 fl oz) lemon juice, or more as desired
salt
2 small carrots, finely sliced
2 raw red beetroots (approximately 160 g /5½ oz),
    peeled and finely chopped
20 g (¾ oz) flat-leaf parsley, snipped
20 sorrel leaves, finely snipped
15 g (½ oz) chopped mint leaves
pepper
approximately 60 ml (2 fl oz) extra-virgin olive oil
4 tablespoons pistachios, toasted and chopped

method

Mix the grated cauliflower with the lemon juice and a pinch of salt. Set aside for 30 minutes.
Add the carrots, beetroots, herbs, pepper and olive oil, making sure
all the ingredients are well coated. Add salt and pepper or lemon juice to taste.
Sprinkle with chopped pistachios and serve immediately.

GUACAMOLE REVISITED

serves 2–4

1 red onion, halved and finely sliced

2 quantities of simple vinaigrette (p. 152)
    replacing the vinegar with lemon juice

the slivered zest of 3 limes, plus juice as desired

pepper

1 garlic clove, peeled and crushed

1 medium red chilli, deseeded and finely chopped

2 tomatoes, diced

1 generous handful of coriander (cilantro)

6 romaine lettuce leaves, torn

2 avocados

salt

method

Soak the onion in water for 10 minutes, then drain well.
In a salad bowl, mix the vinaigrette, lime zest, pepper, garlic and chilli.
Add the tomatoes, coriander, lettuce and drained onion. Toss to coat with dressing.
Peel the avocados, remove the stones and cut into slices, then incorporate them gently
into the salad. Add lime juice, salt and pepper to taste. Serve immediately.

PEACH, TOMATO & MOZZARELLA

124

serves 2–4

4 ripe but firm tomatoes
salt
4 yellow peaches
the juice of 1 lemon, or as desired
1 ball of mozzarella (approximately 125 g/4½ oz)
olive oil
pepper
1 handful of basil leaves

125

method

Cut the tomatoes into thin slices, sprinkle with salt and arrange in a dish. Peel the peaches,
cut into narrow segments and add to the tomatoes. Pour the lemon juice over.
Add the mozzarella, torn or whole, and a dash of olive oil.
Season with salt and pepper to taste. Sprinkle with basil leaves and serve immediately.

CARROT & PISTACHIO

serves 2–4

300 g (11 oz) carrots cut into
    julienne strips

4 tablespoons toasted pistachios

60 g (2 oz) raisins

40 g (1½ oz) coriander (cilantro), roughly chopped

1 quantity of Middle Eastern dressing (p. 158)

salt and pepper

method

Put the carrots, pistachios, raisins and coriander into a salad
bowl, then pour over enough dressing to coat them.
Season with salt and pepper to taste.
Set aside for 15 minutes before serving to allow the flavours to mingle.

WATERMELON & FENNEL

128

serves 2–4

800 g (1 lb 10 oz) watermelon, cut into chunks

100 g (3½ oz) fennel bulb, finely sliced

90 ml (3 fl oz) lime juice

2 green jalapeño peppers, finely chopped

2 tablespoons olive oil

1 teaspoon honey

1 handful of mint, snipped,
   plus a few leaves for garnish

salt and pepper

method

Place the watermelon chunks and fennel in a large salad bowl.
Combine the other ingredients to make a dressing, then pour
over enough to coat the watermelon and fennel.
Serve this salad nice and cool, sprinkled with mint leaves, and seasoned with salt and pepper.

TOMATOES IN VINCOTTO

130

serves 2–4

700 g (1 lb 8 oz) tomatoes in assorted varieties, sizes and colours

salt

1½ tablespoons vincotto (concentrated, slow-cooked
   grape must from Puglia in Italy) or balsamic vinegar

60 ml (2 fl oz) olive oil

2 teaspoons red wine vinegar

1 small handful of lovage or celery leaves

pepper

method

Slice the large tomatoes into crosswise rounds and halve or quarter the small ones.
Arrange them in a salad bowl and sprinkle with salt, then set aside for 10 minutes.
In the meantime, combine the vincotto or balsamic vinegar, oil and red wine vinegar.
Sprinkle the lovage or celery leaves over the tomatoes and pour over enough dressing
to coat them. Add salt and pepper, olive oil or vincotto to taste. Serve immediately.

THAI SALAD WITH PEANUT DRESSING

132

serves 2–4

200 g (7 oz) cooked chicken, thinly sliced

150 g (5 oz) cucumber, cut into julienne strips

65 g (2 oz) crisp salad leaves

40 g (1½ oz) beansprouts

2 hard-boiled eggs, halved

½ red (bell) pepper, cut into thin strips

3 spring onions (scallions), sliced lengthways

1 quantity of spicy peanut dressing (p. 170)

2 tablespoons toasted peanuts, roughly chopped

1 red chilli, finely chopped

method

Arrange all the ingredients, except for the peanut dressing, peanuts and chilli, in a dish.
Pour a few spoonfuls of dressing over and sprinkle with the peanuts
and chilli. Serve with the remaining dressing on the side.

FILLED ENDIVES

134

serves 2–4

2 quantities of simple vinaigrette (p. 152)

2 teaspoons honey

100 g (3½ oz) toasted pistachios, finely chopped

30 g (1 oz) flat-leaf parsley, finely snipped

30 g (1 oz) mint leaves, finely snipped

50 g (2 oz) red onion, finely chopped

1 red apple, unpeeled, diced quite finely

30 g (1 oz) dried barberries

salt and pepper

approximately 16 endive or chicory leaves

method

Mix the vinaigrette and honey. In a salad bowl, combine the
pistachios, parsley, mint, onion, apple and barberries.
Pour over enough dressing to coat the ingredients, then season with salt and pepper.
Arrange the endive leaves in a dish and garnish with the pistachio mixture. Serve immediately.

HERBS, CITRUS & SEEDS

serves 2–4

1 quantity of simple vinaigrette (p. 152) made with sherry vinegar

1 large lemon, peeled and cut into segments, membranes removed

1 large orange, peeled and cut into segments, membranes removed

1 generous handful of mint leaves, coarsely chopped

1 generous handful of flat-leaf parsley, coarsely chopped

1 small bunch of dill, coarsely snipped

1 small bunch of tarragon, coarsely snipped

3 tablespoons seeds, such as sunflower, pumpkin, or a mixture

method

Pour the vinaigrette into a salad bowl and add the other ingredients,
except for the seeds. Toss gently to coat with dressing.
Add the seeds and serve immediately.

BROCCOLI, RAISINS & ANCHOVY

138

serves 2–4

a few saffron threads, finely chopped or ground

800 g (1 lb 10 oz) broccoli (florets and stems)

80 g (3 oz) raisins

40 g (1½ oz) pine kernels

2 quantities of simple vinaigrette (p. 152)

4 anchovy fillets in oil, drained and chopped

method

Mix the saffron with a tablespoon of hot water and set aside.
Cut the broccoli into small florets, thinly slice the stalks and arrange
them in a salad bowl. Add the raisins and pine kernels.
Blend the vinaigrette with the saffron water and anchovies until you have a smooth texture.
Pour enough dressing over the salad to coat it and serve immediately.

KALE, TOMATO & CHICKPEAS

140

serves 2–4

3 tablespoons tahini

2 tablespoons lemon juice, or more as desired

½ garlic clove, peeled and crushed

salt and pepper

4 generous handfuls of young kale leaves

30 cherry tomatoes, halved

200 g (7 oz) cooked or canned chickpeas, rinsed and drained

*best in
summer*

method

Combine the tahini, most of the lemon juice, garlic and season with
salt and pepper. Add 50 ml (2 fl oz) cold water and whisk.
Place the kale, tomatoes and chickpeas in a salad bowl, then pour over enough
dressing to coat them. Season with salt and pepper or lemon juice to taste.
Set aside for 15–60 minutes before serving to allow the flavours to mingle.

FLORENTINE SALAD

serves 2–4

2 quantities of simple vinaigrette (p. 152)

1 garlic clove, peeled and crushed

2 anchovy fillets in oil, drained and thinly sliced

700 g (1 lb 8 oz) nicely ripe tomatoes

1 large cucumber, halved
    lengthwise, then cut into rounds

150 g (5 oz) herby croutons (p. 174)

1 generous handful of basil leaves

salt and pepper

method

Mix the vinaigrette, garlic and anchovies.
Dice the tomatoes and put them in a sieve over a container.
Press with the back of a spoon. Incorporate the juice into the vinaigrette.
Arrange the tomatoes, cucumber, croutons and basil in a salad bowl.
Pour over enough dressing to coat them, then season with salt and pepper to taste.
Set aside for 15–60 minutes before serving to allow the flavours to mingle.

RADISHES & HERB YOGHURT

144

serves 2–4

120 g (4 oz) Greek-style yoghurt

20 ml (¾ fl oz) olive oil

2 garlic cloves, peeled and crushed

4 tablespoons flat-leaf parsley, snipped

12 sorrel leaves, finely chopped

salt and pepper

280 g (10 oz) radishes cut into thin slices

lemon juice, as desired

method

Mix the yoghurt, oil, garlic and herbs in a salad bowl
and season with salt and pepper.
Incorporate the radishes. Add the lemon juice,
as well as salt and pepper to taste. Serve cool.

CUCUMBER & SEAWEED

146

serves 2–4

30 g (1 oz) dried seaweed

1 teaspoon salt

2 medium cucumbers, peeled and cut into strips
    using a peeler or mandoline

4 tablespoons rice vinegar

1 tablespoon caster (superfine) sugar

1 tablespoon dashi (Japanese stock)

1 teaspoon sesame oil

½ teaspoon soy sauce

1 teaspoon black sesame seeds

method

Soak the seaweed in water for 20 minutes, then drain
and thinly slice, removing any hard parts. Rinse and drain again.
Sprinkle salt over the cucumbers and set aside for 10 minutes. Rinse and dab off
any surplus water. Blend all the other ingredients, except for the sesame seeds.
Arrange the seaweed and cucumber in a salad bowl, and pour over enough
dressing to coat them. Sprinkle with sesame seeds and serve.

BRUSSELS SPROUTS & PEAR

148

serves 2–4

2 quantities of simple vinaigrette (p. 152) made with lemon juice

2 teaspoons runny honey

400 g (14 oz) Brussels sprouts, in fine strips,
   ideally cut with a mandoline

80 g (3 oz) pecan nuts, chopped

40 g (1½ oz) goji berries

1 large pear or 2 small firm pears

salt and pepper

149

method

Mix the vinaigrette and honey and set aside.
Combine the Brussels sprouts, pecan nuts and goji berries.
Cut the pear(s) horizontally into fine slices, ideally using a mandoline,
then cut into matchsticks. Add them to the sprouts. Drizzle with vinaigrette, then
season with a generous amount of salt and pepper. Serve immediately.

DRESSINGS
& SECRET TOPPINGS

Dressing is one of the key elements of a good salad.
It is what brings all the ingredients together. To mix the dressing
ingredients well, use a jar with a lid, or whisk until fully combined.
Garnishes are a quick and easy way to dress a salad
by adding delicious flavour and texture.

SIMPLE VINAIGRETTE

makes approximately 50 ml (2 fl oz)

2 tablespoons vegetable oil

1 tablespoon white wine vinegar

1 tablespoon olive oil

½ teaspoon Dijon mustard

salt and pepper

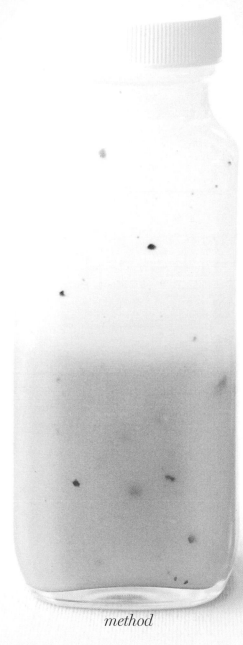

method

Put all the ingredients into a screw-top jar and shake vigorously until blended well.
Variations: add finely snipped herbs such as tarragon or chives, or even finely sliced shallots.
Use different vinegars or lemon juice. This dressing keeps
perfectly in the refrigerator for several days.

YOGHURT WITH A TWIST

154

makes approximately 120 g (4 oz)

100 g (3½ oz) Greek yoghurt
½ teaspoon smoked paprika
1 garlic clove, peeled and crushed
finely chopped zest and the juice of ½ a lemon, or more as desired
1 tablespoon olive oil
½ teaspoon ground cumin
salt and pepper

method

Put all the ingredients into a screw-top jar and shake vigorously until blended well.
Variations: add snipped coriander (cilantro) or replace the paprika and cumin with
chopped herbs such as chives, flat-leaf parsley, mint, chervil, oregano or thyme.

THAI VINAIGRETTE

makes approximately 45 ml (2 fl oz)

2 tablespoons yuzu (Japanese citrus fruit) or lime juice

1 tablespoon toasted sesame oil

½ tablespoon nuoc mâm fish sauce

½ tablespoon palm or soft brown sugar

1 medium red chilli, thinly sliced

1 crushed garlic clove

method

Put all the ingredients into a screw-top jar and shake vigorously until blended well.
This dressing keeps perfectly in the refrigerator for several days.

MIDDLE EASTERN

makes approximately 75 ml (3 fl oz)

4 tablespoons olive oil

2 tablespoons lemon juice

½ teaspoon mild smoked paprika

½ teaspoon ground cumin

½ tablespoon ground sumac

1 garlic clove, peeled and crushed

salt

method

Put all the ingredients into a screw-top jar and shake vigorously until blended well.
This dressing keeps perfectly in the refrigerator for several days.

MAYONNAISE

160

makes approximately 300 ml (10 fl oz)

2 egg yolks

1 tablespoon lemon juice, or more as desired

1 large pinch of salt, or more as desired

250 ml (8 fl oz) vegetable oil

2 tablespoons olive oil

1 heaped teaspoon Dijon mustard

method

Beat the egg yolks with the lemon juice and salt with an electric whisk or
manually until you have a creamy texture. Add the oils gradually in a thin stream,
beating continuously until the mixture is thick and pale yellow in colour.
Incorporate the mustard and add lemon juice or salt to taste.
Keep chilled until serving.

YUZU

makes approximately 120 ml (4 fl oz)

90 ml (3 fl oz) grapeseed oil or other neutral oil

3 tablespoons yuzu (Japanese citrus fruit) juice or lemon juice

½ garlic clove, peeled and crushed

salt and pepper

method

Put all the ingredients into a screw-top jar and shake vigorously until blended well.
This dressing keeps perfectly in the refrigerator for several days.

MISO & GINGER

164

makes approximately 110 ml (4 fl oz)

60 ml (2 fl oz) vegetable oil

2 tablespoons lemon juice

2 tablespoons white miso

1 tablespoon rice vinegar

1 teaspoon toasted sesame oil

1 teaspoon fresh ginger, grated

1 spring onion (scallion), finely chopped

½ teaspoon shoyu or low-salt soy sauce

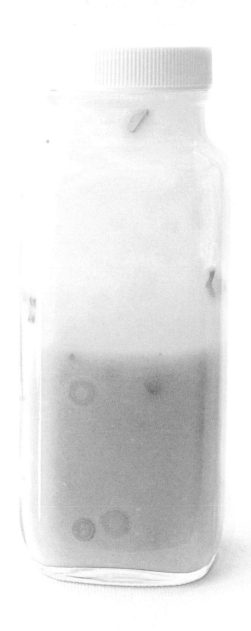

method

Put all the ingredients into a screw-top jar and shake vigorously until blended well.
This dressing keeps perfectly in the refrigerator for several days.

ANCHOVY

makes approximately 100 ml (3 fl oz)

1 quantity of simple vinaigrette (p. 152)
3 anchovy fillets in oil, drained and finely chopped
1 egg yolk
2 tablespoons grated Parmesan

method

Put the vinaigrette and anchovies into a screw-top jar and
shake vigorously until the anchovies come apart.
Add the egg yolk and Parmesan and shake until you have a smooth mixture.

LIME & CHILLI

168

makes approximately 90 ml (3 fl oz)

1 shallot, finely chopped

4 tablespoons chopped coriander (cilantro)

1 tablespoon green jalapeño peppers, finely chopped

2 tablespoons olive oil

2 tablespoons Greek yoghurt

2 tablespoons lime juice

½ garlic clove, peeled and crushed

pepper

method

Put all the ingredients into a screw-top jar and shake vigorously until blended well.
This dressing keeps perfectly in the refrigerator for several days.

SPICY PEANUT DRESSING

makes approximately 300 ml (8 fl oz)

120 ml (4 fl oz) vegetable oil

60 ml (2 fl oz) rice vinegar

75 g (2½ oz) peanut butter

20 ml (¾ fl oz) soy sauce

2 or 3 tablespoons sweet chilli sauce

2 teaspoons fresh ginger, grated

2 tablespoons chopped coriander (cilantro)

2 teaspoons toasted sesame oil

1 tablespoon lime juice, or more as desired

salt and pepper

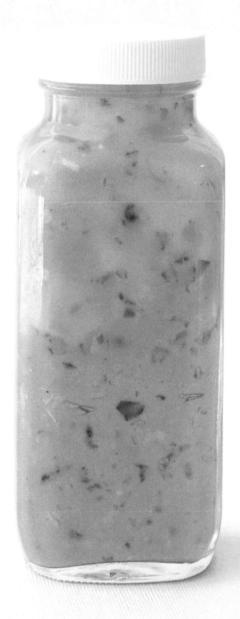

method

Put all the ingredients into a large screw-top jar and shake
vigorously until the peanut butter is well blended.
Add salt and pepper or lime juice to taste.
This dressing keeps perfectly in the refrigerator for several days.

HONEYED NUTS

172

serves 4

100 g (3½ oz) walnuts, pecan nuts, cashew nuts, hazelnuts,
    almonds or a mixture
2 tablespoons honey
2 teaspoons salt
½ teaspoon mild smoked paprika
½ teaspoon ground cinnamon
½ teaspoon Cayenne pepper

method

Preheat the oven to 150°C (300°F/Gas 2).
Mix all the ingredients to coat the nuts in honey and spices. Spread them
on a baking tray lined with greaseproof paper and bake for 15 – 20 minutes,
stirring halfway through. The nuts should be golden but not burnt.
Leave to cool, then chop roughly and sprinkle over the finished salad.

HERBY CROUTONS

174

serves 4

200 g (7 oz) sourdough or farmhouse bread, or ciabatta,
   cut into 1.5 cm (½ in) cubes
100 ml (3 fl oz) melted butter, duck fat or olive oil
2 tablespoons herbs, such as oregano,
   thyme, flat-leaf parsley or a mixture, snipped
1 garlic clove, peeled and crushed
salt and pepper

method

Preheat the oven to 180°C (350°F/Gas 4).
Combine all the ingredients and spread them on a baking tray. Bake for
10 – 15 minutes until the croutons are crunchy and golden.
Leave to cool before adding to the salad.

SPICY CHICKPEAS

serves 4

120 g (4 oz) cooked or canned chickpeas, drained and rinsed

2 tablespoons olive oil

½ teaspoon cayenne pepper

½ teaspoon mild smoked paprika

salt and pepper

method

Dry the chickpeas and rub them vigorously with kitchen towel to remove the skin.
Fry them in the olive oil for 10 minutes or until crunchy and golden. Drain
on kitchen towel, then put in a bowl and mix with the spices and season with salt and pepper.
Leave to cool before sprinkling over the finished salad.

DUKKAH

makes approximately 120 g (4 oz)

30 g (1 oz) hulled hazelnuts or blanched almonds

30 g (1 oz) pistachio kernels

4 tablespoons sesame seeds

2 tablespoons coriander seeds

2 tablespoons cumin seeds

1 teaspoon black peppercorns

2 teaspoons dried thyme

1 teaspoon mild smoked paprika

1 teaspoon salt

method

Lightly toast the hazelnuts and pistachios in a frying pan,
then place them in the bowl of a food processor.
Lightly toast the seeds and peppercorns, then add them to the hazelnuts and pistachios.
Add the thyme, paprika and salt to the food processor bowl
and blend until you have a coarse mixture.
Leave to cool before sprinkling over the finished salad.

PARMESAN TUILES

makes approximately 12 tuiles

50 g (2 oz) finely grated parmesan

method

Preheat the oven to 200°C (400°F/Gas 6).
Line a baking tray with greaseproof paper. Place heaped tablespoons
of parmesan on the tray and flatten with the back of a spoon.
Put in the oven for 3 minutes or until the tuiles turn pale yellow.
Leave them to rest on the tray for a few minutes then slide onto a wire rack
to crisp up. Break into pieces and sprinkle onto the finished salad.

THYME MUESLI

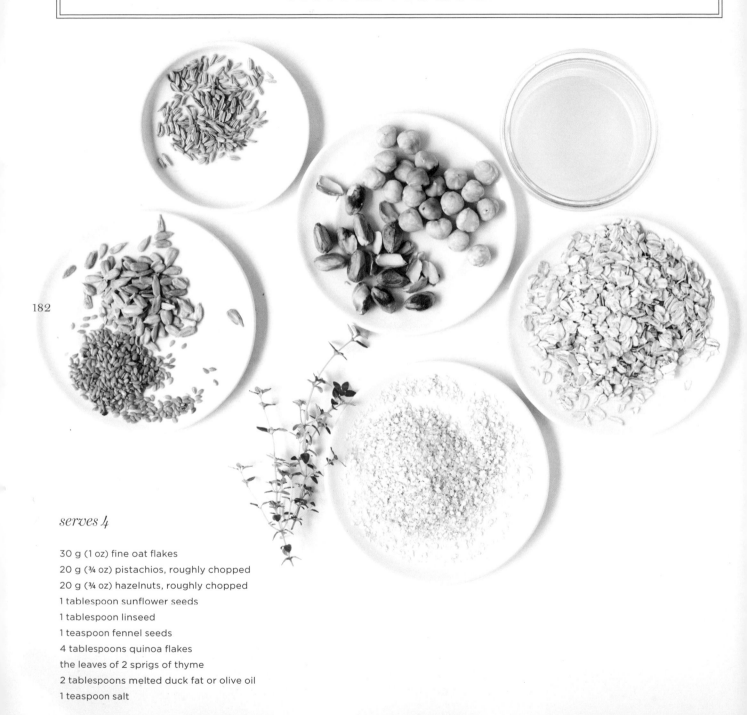

182

serves 4

30 g (1 oz) fine oat flakes

20 g (¾ oz) pistachios, roughly chopped

20 g (¾ oz) hazelnuts, roughly chopped

1 tablespoon sunflower seeds

1 tablespoon linseed

1 teaspoon fennel seeds

4 tablespoons quinoa flakes

the leaves of 2 sprigs of thyme

2 tablespoons melted duck fat or olive oil

1 teaspoon salt

method

Preheat the oven to 150°C (300°F/Gas 2).
Combine all the ingredients and spread them on a baking tray lined with greaseproof
paper. Put in the oven for 25 minutes, keeping a close eye on it and stirring every
10 minutes: the mixture should be very lightly golden and slightly crunchy.
Leave to cool before sprinkling over the finished salad.

CITRUS SALT

makes approximately 30 g (1 oz)

the zest of 8 lemons, finely chopped
the zest of 8 limes, finely chopped
the zest of 4 oranges, finely chopped
2 tablespoons salt

method

Combine all the zests and spread them over a baking tray lined with baking parchment.
Leave in the oven with just the light on for 6 to 8 hours until the
the zest is dry and crunchy. Do not turn the oven on.
You can also spread the zest on a piece of greaseproof paper
and set aside for 24 hours until dry and crunchy.
When the zest is dry, add the salt and store in an airtight container.

CRUNCHY SEEDS IN SOY SAUCE

186

serves 4

80 g (3 oz) assorted seeds, such as
   pumpkin and sunflower
4 tablespoons shoyu or low-salt soy sauce

method

Lightly toast the seeds in a large frying pan over a medium-high heat.
Add the soy sauce, stirring constantly until it boils and evaporates.
Spread the seeds on a sheet of greaseproof paper and leave to cool. Store in an airtight container.

GARLIC CRUMBLE

188

serves 4–6

1 garlic clove, peeled and crushed

2 tablespoons olive oil

4 heaped tablespoons breadcrumbs

3 tablespoons chopped walnuts

the zest of ½ lemon, finely chopped

3 tablespoons mint leaves, snipped

salt and pepper

method

Heat the garlic in the olive oil until it just begins to change colour. Add the breadcrumbs
and walnuts and sauté until golden and crunchy. Remove from the heat.
Add the zest, mint, salt and pepper, as desired.
Leave to cool then sprinkle on the finished salad.

INDEX

191

Thank you to Catie Ziller and all his team, who transformed a simple idea into a magnificent work. I would also like to express my gratitude to Vivian for his fabulous ideas, and also Victoria for her stunning photographs. A thousand thanks also to Elysse for her creative talents that enhance every page of this book.

I would also like to thank lookslikewhite for their superb rammekins and dishes, which can be found on lookslikewhite.com. Canvas Home, ABS Carpet & Home and West Elm, Los Angeles, also provided me with other charming kitchenware.

A big thank you to Magimix UK for the loan of their CS 5200XL food processor, a true workhorse which has saved me hours of chopping and slicing. I must admit that these tasks would have been a real chore without it.

Finally, I am indebted to my family, Adam, Ruby and Ben: they helped me along the way, patiently ate plates and plates of salad and gave me extremely useful suggestions between bites. I love you.

First published in 2015 by Hachette Books (Marabout)
This English language edition published in 2016 by Hardie Grant Books

Hardie Grant Books (UK)
52-54 Southwark Street
London SE1 1UN
hardiegrant.co.uk

Hardie Grant Books (Australia)
Ground Floor, Building 1
658 Church Street
Melbourne, VIC 3121
hardiegrant.com.au

British Library Cataloguing-in-Publication Data. A catalogue record
for this book is available from the British Library.

ISBN: 978-1-78488-036-1

Publisher: Kate Pollard
Senior Editor: Kajal Mistry
Editorial Assistant: Hannah Roberts
Translator: Gilla Evans
Typesetter: David Meikle
Photographer: Victoria Wall Harris
Copy Editor: Nicola Lovick
Graphic design: Elysse Ricci Achuff
Colour Reproduction by p2d

Printed and bound in China by 1010

10 9 8 7 6 5 4 3 2 1